STUDY GUIDE

40,000 W**RDS**

GOD'S
HEART
FOR
YOUR
HOME

about

MARRIAGE & PARENTING

ISBN: 978-1-957369-35-8   1 2 3 4 5 6 7 8 9 10

Printed in the United States of America

STUDY GUIDE

40,000 WORDS

GOD'S HEART FOR YOUR HOME

about

MARRIAGE & PARENTING

SHANNON O'DELL

FO UR

CONTENTS

40,000 W RDS

GOD'S
HEART
FOR
YOUR
HOME

about

MARRIAGE &
PARENTING

SHANNON O'DELL

THE HEART OF MARRIAGE CHAMBER I—LOVE

"If you feel it's impossible to love your spouse right now, I get that. But that's because you're trying to love in your own strength rather than letting Christ love through you with His love."

As you read
Chapter 1:
"Chamber I—
Love" in *40,000
Words About
Marriage and
Parenting*,
reflect on the
questions and
scriptures.

REFLECT AND TAKE ACTION:

How do you show love to your spouse? How
do they show love to you?

J+C: Words of acknowledgement
Say I love you. - doing dishes
-trying to help out around house
* need to do this more. Acts of service

How can you make your love for your
spouse known today?

J+C - Grilling out + doing dishes

How often do you carve out time to spend
with your spouse one-on-one?

J+C - Not as much as I should
- need to figure this out

> *"Dear friends, let us love one another, for love comes from God. Everyone who loves has been born of God and knows God. Whoever does not love does not know God, because God is love. This is how God showed his love among us: He sent his one and only Son into the world that we might live through him."*
>
> *1 John 4:7-9 (NIV)*

Consider the scripture above and answer the following questions:

Who do you think God expects us to love?

Everyone

How can we continue to show love to others even when they hurt us?

By being Kind

What or who is at the center of your marriage? What is your foundation?

God

Look over the "Ten ways a man can honor a woman" and the "Ten ways a woman can honor a man" sections. Of these ten points, which do you personally need to work on? List them below.

JB 1) Date Her 2) Serve her
3) tell her

What are some of the things you love most about your spouse? List them below and share them with your loved one.

JB → How proud I am of her for what she is and has become in Christ.
— She makes me want to do better.
— Physically — everything, every then of her body. She is without flaws in my eyes!

How often do you pray with your spouse? Take time today to pray over the content discussed in this section together.

JB— try to at Night but I need to get better

CHAPTER 2

THE HEART OF MARRIAGE CHAMBER II—FORGIVENESS

"Thank God for his forgiveness; forgive others, and seek forgiveness from others. Because when sin tries to kill your intimacy, you can put it to death on the cross time after time after time with forgiveness."

REFLECT AND TAKE ACTION:

Do you ever have trouble forgiving your spouse for something they did or didn't do? Do they ever have trouble forgiving you? How does this struggle play out practically in your marriage?

_____

_____

_____

_____

_____

_____

What does forgiveness mean to you? Does God have the same definition?

_____

_____

_____

_____

_____

_____

After you you've forgiven your partner or been forgiven, do you feel that you are closer as a couple? How so?

_____

_____

_____

_____

_____

_____

Consider the scripture above and answer the following questions:

Have you ever struggled to forgive someone who wronged you or hurt you in the past? Describe your experience.

_____

_____

_____

_____

_____

Why should we be quick to forgive and not harbor bitterness, rage, and anger against others?

_____

_____

_____

_____

_____

Have you ever had trouble asking for forgiveness or admitting that you've done something wrong? Has your partner? Describe a relevant experience you've had in the past.

_____

_____

_____

_____

Do you think that transparency is an essential component of forgiveness? Why or why not?

_____

_____

_____

_____

_____

Take time to ponder and list ways you feel that you have wronged your spouse. Then, share your list with them and ask for forgiveness.

_____

_____

_____

_____

_____

How do you think a relationship will fare if both parties never ask for forgiveness? What will happen in such a relationship?

_____

_____

_____

_____

_____

CHAPTER 3

THE HEART OF MARRIAGE CHAMBER III— COMMUNICATION

Great communication isn't about getting our way; it's about doing it God's way."

READING TIME

As you read Chapter 3: "Chamber III—Communication" in *40,000 Words About Marriage and Parenting,* reflect on the questions and scriptures.

REFLECT AND TAKE ACTION:

How strong do you feel the communication in your marriage is on a scale of 1-10? What can you personally do to improve this number?

_____

_____

_____

_____

_____

_____

What happens to a relationship if there is no communication—or improper communication?

_____

_____

_____

_____

_____

_____

Do you communicate only to negotiate and get your way, or to reach common understanding? How do you know?

_____

_____

_____

_____

_____

"Therefore each of you must put off falsehood and speak truthfully to your neighbor, for we are all members of one body. 'In your anger do not sin': Do not let the sun go down while you are angry, and do not give the devil a foothold."

Ephesians 4:25-27 (NIV)

Consider the scripture above and answer the following questions:

Have you ever let the sun go down while you were angry, as this verse states not to do? Describe the experience. What was the outcome?

_____

_____

_____

_____

How do you think lack of communication—or improper communication—"gives the devil a foothold" in our relationships?

_____

_____

_____

_____

Are you guilty of communicating when you feel any of the H.A.L.T. symptoms discussed (Hungry, Angry, Lonely, Tired)? How did these feelings affect your ability to effectively communicate with others?

_____

_____

_____

_____

Have you and your partner ever communicated with/through a therapist or mediator? If so, how was the experience in your opinion? If not, is there something stopping you?

_____

_____

_____

_____

_____

_____

Read Philippians 1:1-11 independently and discuss your reactions to the passage with your partner. What do you feel God is trying to tell each of you through this text?

_____

_____

_____

_____

_____

_____

How do you feel you can improve your communication with your partner? How do you feel that your partner can improve their communication with you? Take time to share your answers, and pray together for God's assistance in growing closer through healthy communication.

_____

_____

_____

_____

_____

_____

THE HEART OF MARRIAGE
CHAMBER IV—RED-HOT SEX

"If there is any question in your mind that God intended sex to be free, frequent, pleasurable and highly erotic, look no further than the Bible."

READING
TIME

As you read
Chapter 4:
"Chamber IV—
Red-Hot Sex"
in *40,000 Words
About Marriage
and Parenting*,
reflect on the
questions and
scriptures.

REFLECT AND TAKE ACTION:

Are you currently satisfied with you and your partner's sex life? Do you think your partner feels the same way? Why or why not?

_____

_____

_____

_____

_____

_____

Do you feel that your marriage can exist without ingredient? Why or why not?

_____

_____

_____

_____

_____

_____

Did anything from mentioned from God's Word, and His expectations of sexual intimacy between husband and wife, stick out to you from this chapter? If so, what was it?

_____

_____

_____

_____

_____

_____

> *"Do not deprive each other except perhaps by mutual consent and for a time, so that you may devote yourselves to prayer. Then come together again so that Satan will not tempt you because of your lack of self-control."*
>
> *1 Corinthians 7:5 (NIV)*

Consider the scripture above and answer the following questions:

In your own words, what is this verse speaking to in a marriage? Why is this so essential?

_____

_____

_____

_____

_____

According to this verse, how can Satan tempt us as couples? What can we do to prevent this?

_____

_____

_____

_____

_____

What can you do personally to improve your partner's experience? What's holding you back from doing so, if anything?

_____

_____

_____

_____

_____

Consider the methods of emotional and material adultery listed in this chapter. Between yourself and God, are you guilty of any of them? Take time to consider them all and be open in communication with your spouse about what you find.

_____

_____

_____

_____

Why do you think communication and sexual intimacy are so dependent upon one another? Have you ever found yourself in the "No Sex? No Talk. No Talk? No Sex." Cycle?

_____

_____

_____

_____

What are some tangible steps you can take to improve you and your spouse's sexual intimacy? List them below and share them with your partner. Come up with a plan to improve each other's experience and commit to seeing it through.

_____

_____

_____

_____

THE HEART OF PARENTING CHAMBER I—LOVE

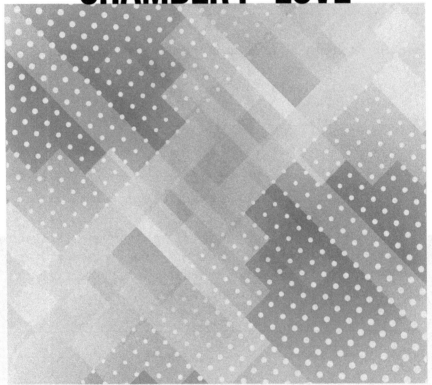

*"If you love [Jesus] with real love,
everything else will follow."*

READING TIME

As you read Chapter 5: "Chamber I— Love" in *40,000 Words About Marriage and Parenting*, reflect on the questions and scriptures.

REFLECT AND TAKE ACTION:

What kind of quality time do you spend with your children?

_____

_____

_____

_____

_____

_____

_____

Do you think it's important to put your love for Jesus first? Why?

_____

_____

_____

_____

_____

_____

_____

Have you ever been hurt by a decision your child made or by something they said? What was it? Why did this hurt you?

_____

_____

_____

_____

_____

_____

> *"Jesus replied, 'Anyone who loves me will obey my teaching. My Father will love them, and we will come to them and make our home with them. Anyone who does not love me will not obey my teaching. These words you hear are not my own; they belong to the Father who sent me."*
>
> *John 14:23-24 (NIV)*

Consider the scripture above and answer the following questions:

What practically happens when we put our love for Jesus first?

_____

_____

_____

_____

_____

If we love Jesus enough to obey His teaching, how will we treat those around us?

_____

_____

_____

_____

_____

Are you vulnerable and humble in front of your children? Why do you think this is important?

_____

_____

_____

_____

_____

How do you handle your children making bad decisions? Do you punish them or try to guide them? Which strategy is more effective?

_____

_____

_____

_____

_____

What parenting principles from this chapter stood out to you? Which do you need to work on?

_____

_____

_____

_____

_____

In what new ways can you express your love to your children? When can you do this? What would it look like?

_____

_____

_____

_____

_____

THE HEART OF PARENTING CHAMBER II—HONOR

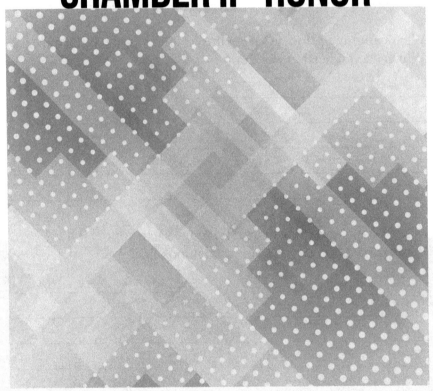

"Honor puts value on something. Honor makes something exceptional. We dishonor something by treating it as usual or common, and that's what so many of us do with God today."

READING
TIME

As you read
Chapter 6:
"Chamber II—
Honor" in
*40,000 Words
About Marriage
and Parenting,*
reflect on the
questions and
scriptures.

REFLECT AND TAKE ACTION:

Do you feel that your children honor you?

_____

_____

_____

_____

_____

_____

What does honor mean, in your own words? Do you show God the same honor you expect from your children? How do you know?

_____

_____

_____

_____

_____

_____

Do you feel that your children's honor for you should be dependent upon your decisions and the example you set for them? Why or why not?

_____

_____

_____

_____

_____

_____

> *"Wisdom's instruction is to fear the LORD,*
> *and humility comes before honor."*
>
> *Proverbs 15:33 (NIV)*

Consider the scripture above and answer the following questions:

What is your initial reaction to this verse? According to this, do you fear the Lord?

_____

_____

_____

_____

_____

_____

In what ways does humility come before honor?

_____

_____

_____

_____

_____

Why is humility an essential component of honor?

_____

_____

_____

_____

_____

Think of a time in which your children dishonored you. How did this experience make you feel?

_____

_____

_____

_____

_____

Read John 12:1-19 individually. What stands out to you from this passage? Share your findings as a family.

_____

_____

_____

_____

_____

What are some takeaways you can personally work on from this chapter? Personal humility? Honoring resources? Honoring your kids?

_____

_____

_____

_____

_____

THE HEART OF PARENTING CHAMBER III—TRAINING

"Training your kids starts with this confession: Lord I can't do this, but you can. And you live in me. My life is your life. I'm trusting you to do it through me."

READING TIME

As you read Chapter 7: "Chamber III— Training" in *40,000 Words About Marriage and Parenting*, reflect on the questions and scriptures.

REFLECT AND TAKE ACTION:

How do you teach your children a new and important principle? Do you have a method in place?

_____

_____

_____

_____

_____

_____

Do you think your children learn faster through listening to what you say or by watching what you do? How do you know?

_____

_____

_____

_____

_____

_____

Do you involve God daily and ask for His assistance in your parenting? How might you invite Him even more to be Lord in this area of your life?

_____

_____

_____

_____

_____

_____

> *"I am the vine; you are the branches. If you remain in me and I in you, you will bear much fruit; apart from me you can do nothing."*
>
> *John 15:5 (NIV)*

Consider the scripture above and answer the following questions:

Do you think this verse relates to training your children? Explain.

_____

_____

_____

_____

_____

How can you ensure that you're setting a good example for your children? What will happen in this regard if you do not remain connected to the Vine?

_____

_____

_____

_____

_____

Do you lead intentionally, with initiative, indirectly, and immediately? Which of these principles do you most need to work on in your parenting?

_____

_____

_____

_____

Of the parenting principles in Proverbs discussed in this section, which have you taught your children to date? Which do you still need to impress upon them?

_____

_____

_____

_____

_____

Which principle from this chapter stood out to you the most? How can you turn this principle into an actionable next step in your life?

_____

_____

_____

_____

_____

Look at the concepts from this above question that you still need to teach your children. Make a list you can act on moving forward, along with any practical steps and helpful notes on how to make it happen.

_____

_____

_____

_____

_____

THE HEART OF PARENTING CHAMBER IV—TRUTH

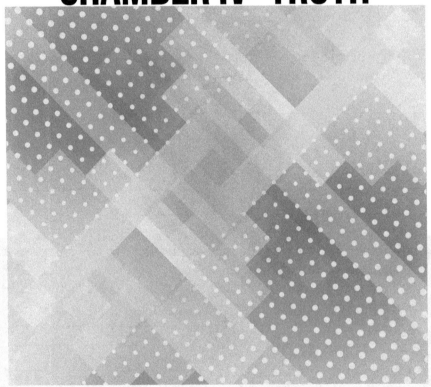

"The Bible is your fuel. It's your nourishment. Don't be thinking that you're passionate about God without being passionate about the Bible."

READING TIME

As you read Chapter 8: "Chamber IV— Truth" in *40,000 Words About Marriage and Parenting*, reflect on the questions and scriptures.

REFLECT AND TAKE ACTION:

What is the foundation of your parenthood? From where does your truth come?

_____

_____

_____

_____

_____

_____

Have you ever felt that the truth of God's Word has been buried amongst your busy lives? If so, describe how you experienced this.

_____

_____

_____

_____

_____

_____

Do you ever spend time with your children in God's Word? If so, do you feel that you spend enough time with them in His Word?

_____

_____

_____

_____

_____

_____

> *"Anyone who lives on milk, being still an infant, is not acquainted with the teaching about righteousness. But solid food is for the mature, who by constant use have trained themselves to distinguish good from evil."*
>
> *Hebrews 5:13-14 (NIV)*

Consider the scripture above and answer the following questions:

What is this verse talking about when it mentions milk and solid food?

_____

_____

_____

_____

_____

Do you believe that God desires for you to delve deeper into His Word than you have to date?

_____

_____

_____

_____

_____

How do you think spending more time in God's Word will affect your parenting?

_____

_____

_____

_____

_____

Meet with your family and take time to individually read Deuteronomy 6:1-9. Have everyone point out what they feel is the most important part of this passage. How can you implement the instructions discussed in these verses?

_____

_____

_____

_____

_____

How do you feel a family will function when they are not rooted in God's Word?

_____

_____

_____

_____

_____

When can you and your family spend time together reading, studying, and praying over His Word regularly? List some times and make a plan to integrate this practice into your routines.

_____

_____

_____

_____

_____